HARLEQUIN'S STICK   *CHARLIE'S CANE*

HARLEQUIN'S———CHARLIE'S
STICK —————CANE

A COMPARATIVE STUDY OF
COMMEDIA DELL' ARTE AND SILENT SLAPSTICK COMEDY.
ILLUSTRATED.

by

David Madden

POPULAR PRESS

A shorter version of *Harlequin's Stick, Charlie's Cane* was delivered
as a lecture at the 1968 meeting of the Society for Cinema Studies
and published in *Film Quarterly*, XXII, No. 1 (Fall, 1968).

"The Virgin of Venice" originally appeared in *Playboy* magazine;
copyright © 1968 by HMH Publishing Co., Inc.

For Russell Green,
who aroused my interest in
Commedia dell' arte

In Memory of Straight Hair and Fatsi
(Laurel and Hardy)

BOOKS BY DAVID MADDEN

Criticism

Wright Morris
James M. Cain
The Poetic Image in Six Genres
Harlequin's Stick, Charlie's Cane
Tough Guy Writers of the Thirties (Editor)
Proletarian Writers of the Thirties (Editor)
American Dreams, American Nightmares (Editor)
Rediscoveries (Editor)
The Popular Culture Explosion (Co-editor)
Nathanael West: The Cheaters and the Cheated (Editor)
Remembering James Agee (Editor)
Creative Choices (Editor)
Studies in the Short Story (Co-editor)
Contemporary Literary Scene (Co-editor)

Fiction

The Beautiful Greed
Cassandra Singing
The Shadow Knows (Short Stories)
Brothers in Confidence
Hair of the Dog
Bijou

David Madden is Writer-in-Residence at Louisiana State University. Born in Knoxville, Tennessee, in 1933, he was educated at the University of Tennessee, San Francisco State College, and Yale Drama School; he has taught English, drama, and creative writing in several universities and colleges, including Centre, the University of Louisville, and Kenyon, where he was also assistant editor of *The Kenyon Review*; he is now an associate editor of *Film Heritage, Film Journal*, and several literary magazines. *The Shadow Knows* was a National Council on the Arts Selection; two of the stories were included in *Best American Short Stories*. His stories, poems, literary essays, and plays have appeared in a wide variety of publications, from popular to literary to avant-garde magazines. Many of his plays have won contests and had productions outside New York City. His latest novel, *Bijou*, is about a thirteen-year-old movie palace usher who wants to be a writer; to work on that novel he received a Rockefeller Grant in 1969.

CONTENTS

INTRODUCTION: THE SPIRIT OF
COMMEDIA RESURRECTED

Most of the best books on the commedia dell'arte appeared in the twenties. Many point out briefly the parallel between commedia dell'arte techniques and those of Chaplin's Tramp. And many writers on silent slapstick films mention this Chaplin-commedia parallel. But I know of no detailed, extended comparison. Academic comparisons are often odious, and contrasts are often irrelevant, but they can instruct and delight, though one always risks seeming to make a hysterical discovery of the obvious. We will get a better perspective on silent slapstick if we look at its major parallel in the past; and there is no better living evidence of what commedia dell'arte was like than American silent slapstick movies.

Certain differences between commedia and silent slapstick raise the question: How can you compare the two

When commedia dell'arte played directly to its audience, whereas silent slapstick reached its audience through a strip of celluloid projected onto a white screen?

When commedia plays were often as long as three hours, whereas silent slapstick movies were comparatively much briefer?

When five commedia characters wore masks whereas the faces of silent slapstick characters were only semi-masks?

When in commedia there was almost constant verbal dexterity, slapstick noise, music, and color, whereas silent slapstick was comparatively mute and black and white?

When the various commedia characters were usually all in the same plays, interacting upon each other as an ensemble, whereas Charlie, Harold, Buster, Ben, Stan, and Oliver usually acted in separate films—as stars (though they may have acted together in early Sennett movies)?

When, except for Harlequin's metempsychosis in Charlie, the commedia stock characters are only vaguely resurrected in silent slapstick characters?

When commedia was not transvisualized through the camera and projector, whereas silent slapstick was?

Even though one sees clearly that both used stereotyped characters and that improvisation based on a sketchy scenario is the pulse of both commedia and silent slapstick?

If despite his masklike deadpan, Buster Keaton is unique, in a vital sense, *all* silent slapstick characters are unique, even Charlie-Harlequin, for what is periodically rejuvenated in comedy is never a mere duplicate of what once died.

A provocative comparison lies not in seeing detailed similarities—between characters, for instance—but in seeing certain character traits, story elements, comic routines, principles, and methods of comedy as common to both.   Since the sound elements in commedia though secondary, make up almost half of the experience, why not, one might ask, focus the comparison on early sound film comedy rather than silent?   Again, the point to stress is that what is resurrected is the *spirit* of commedia, which is most dynamically expressed in the action element and in nonverbal projections of its stock characters.

I. CHARACTER TYPES RESHUFFLED

Commedia dell'arte means comedy of the profession of skill (not of *art*); thus, it contrasted its actors with the numerous amateur actors of the *erudita* or "learned comedy." Italian popular comedy had many other names: improvised comedy, subject comedy, masked comedy, unwritten comedy.

The typical commedia play involved three interacting sets of stock characters. Most important were the professional types.

Pantaloon was an elderly but still vigorous merchant, a native of Venice. A miserly, overreaching, credulous, talkative, sententious old fool, he was the cuckolded husband of a passionate young wife and the deceived father of an eager virgin. Ineffectually amorous himself, he was always outwitted in love by his son, his servant, the Doctor or the Captain. He wore long trousers and slippers turned up at the toes in the Turkish manner. He wore a reddish-brown mask with a hooked nose and spectacles, and a pointed beard.

The Doctor, usually a friend of Pantaloon, was a pretentious, comic man of learning, a product of the University of Bologna. Usually a lawyer, but sometimes a physician, an astrologer, or a professor, he spouted Latin inaccurately and garbled facts into balderdash. Sometimes the father of one of the lovers, he was inclined to pursue women himself. His black mask covered only his forehead, and included a comic nose, and a short, pointed beard. Dressed entirely in black, he wore an academic robe and a gigantic hat.

The third professional type was the military man. The Captain is a carry-over of the Miles Gloriosus figure of ancient Roman comedy, given fresh impetus by the presence in Italy of the Spanish conquerers. When he enters in his flamboyant outift, including a plumed hat, wearing a flesh-colored mask with a Cyrano nose and a fierce mustache, carrying a hideous sword, he creates terror for a moment, swaggering, parading, blustering, threatening, bragging of his feats in love and war, but he dodges if someone sneezes, he flees if someone makes the faintest aggressive gesture.

The two comic servants, or *zanni*, were employed by Pantaloon, the Doctor, or the Captain, but they usually assisted the lovers in scheming against their masters. Just as Pantaloon and the Doctor were companions, Harlequin and his opposite, Brighella, were conspirators or rivals. In fact, originally, lower Bergamo produced the dull-witted Harlequin and upper Bergamo the crafty Brighella. Dishonest, unscrupulous, opportunistic, malicious, vengeful, egotistic, sinister Brighella was a more deliberate caricature of the servant type than Harlequin. Sometimes a hired thug or a thief or a panderer with a prowl-like gait, he would often move the audience by suddenly lapsing into music, dancing, singing, playing the guitar or flute. He wore an olive-tinted mask with "a bizarre, half-cynical, half-mawkish expression . . . sloe eyes, a hook nose, thick and sensual lips, a brutal chin bristling with a sparse beard, and finally the moustache of a fop, thick and twirled at the ends."[1] He wore a jacket and full trousers, decorated with braid, a large leather purse, and a dagger.

Pulcinella (who became the English Punch) was somewhat similar to Brighella; both had many job functions and ultimately became associated with Naples. Hooknosed, hunchbacked, pot-bellied, old but still energetic and pugnacious, Pulchinella walked with a henlike hop, and made little "cheep" sounds. He wore a loose blouse and balloonlike pantaloons of white linen and a white duncelike cap; from his heavy leather belt hung a wooden sword and a large wallet.

A different sort of valet character was Pedrolino, who became the French Pierrot. "He is a young, personable, and trustworthy individual who can be a charming lover"—usually of Colombine, the maid-servant. Though he had an "engaging simplicity and elegance" and "a tenderness and sensitiveness . . . characteristic of the lovers in the aristocratic pastorals of the period," he is still a comic character (Ducharte, 251). He is always looking for something to eat, and often ends up getting beaten by his master. Pierrot's costume is almost as familiar as Harlequin's, but he wears no mask.

A maidservant assisted the Inamorata in her love intrigues, and she often had affairs herself with servants or with the professional types. Colombine (sometimes called Arlecchina) was a coarse, witty, bright counterpart of Harlequin, but was seldom a focal character in the action.

Though most scenarios concerned love intrigues, the lovers themselves were not as important as the professional and the male servant
types. They were somewhat like straight men in vaudeville. Their
dress and speeches imitated the styles and mannerisms of the courtiers. Neither the female servants nor the lovers wore character masks.

While the parallels between these commedia characters and silent slapstick characters are not as close as those between Harlequin and Charlie, we do see traces of Pantaloon in John Bunny, W. C. Fields, even in Oliver Hardy; of the Doctor in Hardy, and in Fields and Groucho Marx after movies learned to talk; of the swaggering, bullying captain in Ford Sterling, Wallace Beery, Fields, and the cop on the beat; of Pedrolino-Pierrot in some of Charlie and Harold Lloyd and in Langdon and Harpo Marx; of Punch in Fields and Ford Sterling; of Columbine and of the Inamorata in the various girls whom the slapstick comics pursue. And if we pair Harlequin and Brighella, we see dimwit Laurel and sly Hardy, the first great comedy team.

But the point is that each commedia character was a special combination of certain traits that became hilarious when activated in patterned relationships with other characters. Reshuffled, these traits turn up in new combinations in important and minor characters and actor-characters in silent slapstick cinema.

II. HARLEQUIN AND CHARLIE: ICONS

Allardyce Nicoll in *The World of Harlequin* notes that "in several recent books on the commedia dell'arte the name of Charlie Chaplin has been familiarly invoked as though he were the living embodiment of this style of theatre. Nothing could be more in error. Everyone recognizes Charlie Chaplin's genius as a pantomimic actor; everyone equally recognizes that his skill evaporates when he turns to dialogue. The truly talented exponents of the commedia dell'arte depended upon both."[2]

Ducharte was one of the first to observe that "though he may
not be aware of it, Charlie Chaplin is undoubtedly one of the rare
inheritors of the traditions of the commedia dell'arte" (219). He
notes that Chaplin's pantomime in *Shoulder Arms* when he poses as
a tree is remarkably like Pulcinella's mimicry of a weathercock whirl-
ing in the wind, then a milestone inert in a garden, then a winnowing
basket, which goes off to the woods pretending to be a tortoise. The
comparison is based not so much upon similarities between Charlie
and Pulcinella as upon a principle of comic business: the contrast
between absolute immobility and sudden agility. Ducharte concludes,
"The sublime Charlie Chaplin has originated a character far more
popular and universal than was Harlequin" (302).

If Nicoll dismisses the comparison too glibly, embraces it too passionately, for Charlie is popular because he is one of the greatest (and unfortunately the most recent) of Harlequin's numerous avatars. Of the many cinema scholars who see the comparison, Roger Manvell is typical in declaring that Harlequin is at the root of Chaplin's art. "The source, the ingenuity, the by-play with vice and virtue, the visual innuendoes"—these make Harlequin-Charlie a character who "will never die or grow old-fashioned."[3]

If as Nicoll says, the two most universally known theatrical characters are Harlequin and Hamlet, a new medium offered in the days of silent slapstick a character even more famous: Charlie. But Hamlet exists in only one play, Harlequin and Charlie in hundreds. Man has no universal image of Hamlet, but distinctive costumes and bodily stances immediately declare Harlequin and Charlie. Harlequin and Charlie are archetypal proletarians, created by the workers. They are again like Hamlet in that it is the intellectuals who keep all three still breathing today. If Harlequin and Charlie seem incapable of keeping more than one idea in their heads at a time, and if thus, for them, as Bazin says, "there is no such thing as the future,"[4] the ability of the intellectual to think, feel, sometimes act, in a timeless world of imagination and of opposing ideas assures Hamlet (who couldn't make up his mind either), Harlequin, and Charlie a place in whatever future they can help us make for ourselves.

What does Harlequin have to say for himself as a character? In
my play *Fugitive Masks*, the actor in the troupe who portrays him
arrogantly argues Harlequin's supremacy and immortality:

The public can be *moved* to applaud only Harlequin! Even the
little playwright, had he enough talent to nurse such an overreaching
ambition, would aspire to play Harlequin. After the characters you
play have passed from the scene, I, in one form or another, but recognizable immediately as Harlequin, will still be leaping like Mercury
through the air. If there is a priest of the Commedia cult, it is I, and
the stage is my temple. No man can but feel a sense of the godlike
playing the mask of Harlequin. It is true that without you, Harlequin
is only an idea in the mind of God. But what an idea! For I was
created by the gods as a drunken lark and fostered by men as a bold
venture of the imagination. Somewhere on the altars of Time, our
phalluses were chopped off, but mine is still potent in my magic bat.
I am the poet of acrobats; my very body laughs. Make my statue of
rubber. I pluck a limp, wrinkled rainbow from my trunk and endow
it with my shape, and beholding it, the world can only rejoice. And
as my costume turns like a crystal, I mirror, in the flash of a single
performance, all the moods man is heir to. A grotesque tatterdemal-
ion of vices and virtues, Harlequin is many things, all wonderful to
behold. Tell me—who *is* Harlequin? A shrewd but ignorant valet,
who serves lovers, and cheats old men. A capering, clumsy, credulous
clown, a rogue, a rake, a blundering, inept fool.

Greedy, ribald, charming, impulsive, malicious, melancholy. Always striking poses, always leaping—like a drunken gazelle. Eternally amorous. Easily hurt, quickly comforted. His grief and his joy equally comic. My origins in man are a mystery, bu I am a divine creation, who at any moment may assume a diabolical stance. But only for a moment. While the rest of you are fixed, though not as frozen as the playwright would like you to be, I am elusive. I am your only hope for avoiding the lethal touch of the playwright's shaping hand. He can never capture and encage me in any play, for it is only in an endless succession of plays that I may be said to exist at all, a human godhead of freedom and possibilities. Who is Harlequin? One can only answer that Harlequin, like his costume, is a puzzle, the pieces in each of you."[5]

Much about the origins of the commedia characters is a mystery. But Chaplin's account of how Charlie the Tramp came into being is like a poetically compressed parable of the spirit that produced commedia characters in Renaissance Italy. Mack Sennett was standing with Mabel Normand, looking into a hotel lobby set. He turned to Charles Chaplin and said, "Put on a comedy make-up. Anything will do." At first Chaplin had no ideas, then "on the way to the wardrobe, I thought I would dress in baggy pants, big shoes, a cane and a derby hat. I wanted everything a contradiction: the pants baggy, the coat tight, the hat small and the shoes large. . . . I added a moustache, which, I reasoned, would add age without hiding my expression.

"I had no idea of the character. But the moment I was dressed, the clothes and the make-up made me feel the person he was. I began to know him, and by the time I walked onto the stage he was fully born. When I confronted Sennett I assumed the character and strutted about swinging my cane and parading before him. Gag and comedy ideas went racing through my mind. . . .

"I began to explain the character. 'You know, this fellow is many-sided, a tramp, a gentleman, a poet, a dreamer, a lonely fellow, always hopeful of romance and adventure. He would have you believe he is a scientist, a musician, a duke, a polo player. Howerver, he is not above picking up a cigarette butt or robbing a baby of its candy. And, of course, if the occasion warrants it, he will kick a lady in the rear—but only in extreme anger!' " The players in the other companies at Keystone, stagehands, carpenters, wardrobe people left their sets to watch. Even Ford Sterling, the studio star, was attracted. "As the clothes had imbued me with the character, I then and there decided I would keep this costume, whatever happened."[6] The whole world knows what happened. It had happened before—in Italy.[7]

As Chaplin draped Charlie in the garb of a convict, clergyman, factory worker, soldier, streetcleaner, millionaire, he demonstrated that constancy of character is more important than costume. Thus he went a step beyond Harlequin, who wore only disguises over his standard costume. In the early days of silent slapsticks, the comic situation submerged the participants; but Chaplin is a supreme example of the comic's progress from object to subject, of the triumph of the individual over the inhuman machinery of farce.

In Harlequin and Charlie, the little man, the underdog, reaches mythic proportions. Unlike other legendary, literary, and theatrical figures of universal fame—Robin Hood, Roland, Hamlet, Ulysses, Estrogon—they have no literary memorial. They are poetic images. Harlequin is seen only in icons; Charlie still moves on the screen, though in no new guises. Thus, Charlie the encumbered dancer also is an immortal figure on an urn.

III. LIMITATIONS (1)

It is in those characteristics which set them apart from other kinds of comedy that commedia and silent slapstick are alike and unlike. And it is from these unique characteristics that they derive their triumphs, for each characteristic is an externally imposed or self-imposed limitation forcing the actor to develop skills that enable him to control and turn to advantage those limitations. Convention imposed upon the commedia the limitation of the five masks. Technology imposed upon slapstick cinema the limitation of silence. The commedia imposed upon itself the tasks of improvised action and dialogue. Silent slapstick imposed upon itself the limitation of improvised action, which had the added burden of compensating for lack of sound.

IV. THE SCENARIOS: FREEDOM WITH RISKS

If there were conventional limitations in commedia dell'arte and technological limitations in silent slapstick, both had one basic source of freedom—the sketchy scenarios. But it was a freedom that entailed risk and imposed responsibilities upon the actors.

A skeleton scenario hung backstage. On a narrow stage, against a crude curtain, the actors wove its flesh and gave it pulse. The some 800 scenarios that have been preserved are sketchy—the ones that haven't been were perhaps even less detailed.[8] Some commedia scholars envision the manager dashing one off on his knee. In the early days of Keystone, Mack Sennett, as he explained to film novice Charles Chaplin, used no scenario at all: "We get an idea, then follow the natural sequence of events until it leads up to a chase, which is the essence of our comedy" (Chaplin, 141). Perhaps this is what is known as "shooting off the cuff." One wonders whether the person who first used the term *scenario* on a movie lot knew its ancestry.

The commedia manager, and usually the chief actor as well, wrote the scenarios, with some help from the other actors; he stole as much material as he could. Mack Sennett wrote scenarios before his Keystone days, and confesses that he lifted his first one from O. Henry. Sennett also was an actor. Arthur Knight says Sennett was "possessed by a consuming ambition; he wanted to play a comic policeman."[9] Father Goose, as Gene Fowler calls him, multiplied his ambition vicariously by creating the Keystone Kops. With the help of his gag men, he thought up most of the Keystone antics. A one-man audience, he let his troupe know how well he and they had used their unscripted freedom by the creak of his rocking chair in the rear of the screening room; his troupe listened to the speed of the rocking as a way of measuring Sennett's excitement.

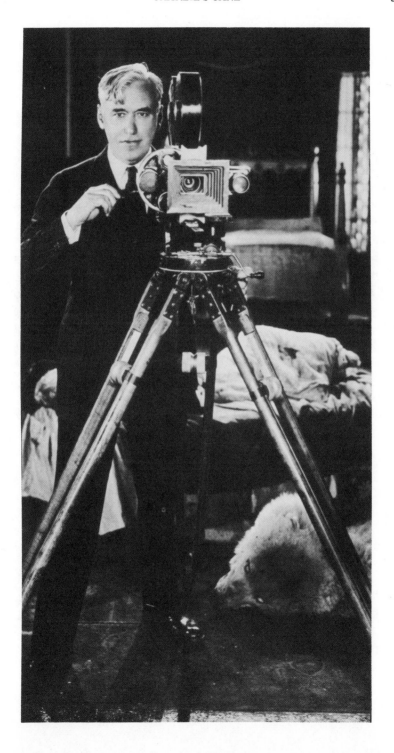

The most frequent narrative line in both commedia and silent slapstick concerned love intrigues. The commedia love plots were often extremely complex, sometimes involving three sets of lovers, whose efforts were further complicated by the erotic overreaching of Pantaloon, the Captain, Harlequin, and Columbine—each person in love with someone else, all acting at cross-purposes, entangled in misunderstandings and mistaken identities. Silent slapstick simplified all this into the struggle of a single comic character to win one girl. In Charlie and other slapstick comics, Harlequin is combined with the courtly lover. Alone, the courtly lover as a type has, of course, no parallel in our silent slapstick, though he reappears in the musical comedies of the thirties and forties, with their romantic subplots. The zannis—Laurel and Hardy or the Marx Brothers—become matchmakers, though one of the comics, Laurel, for instance, may be in love with the beautiful girl.

In silent slapstick the beautiful girls sometimes became in later years straight serious lovers: Jean Harlow, Paulette Goddard, Carole Lombard, Joan Crawford, Gloria Swanson, Edna Purviance.

Mabel Normand, queen of the slapstick beauties, shared many of the talents of the male comics. A carefree sprite, a tomboy, a Cinderella, she was capable of provoking many moods, from violent slapstick to pathos. If we compare the early commedia company the Gelosi with Keystone, Mabel Normand certainly parallels the celebrated actress Isabella. But she, like most of the silent heroines, combines the Isabella type of Inamorata with the maidservant Colombine; many of the silent heroines were working girls.

Though at times female impersonators were used, commedia
brought women onto the stage on almost equal terms with the men.
Slapstick comedy companies were democratic clearing houses for
the emancipated young girl, recently freed from Victorian restraint,
so that in Mabel Normand the reincarnated Renaissance Isabella
experienced new freedoms and a less conventionalized character
style. The famous Keystone bathing beauties, prefigured in the
ballerinas of the commedia, were one manifestation of the new sex-
ual freedom.

The chaste love of the virginal lovers had its farcical erotic side in the vulgarity of the old men and of the servants. The drawings that have come down to us show Harlequin with his hand up Colombine's dress or fondling her bare breasts. Pantaloon prances about sporting an enormous phallus. Such ostentatiousness deserves to be deflated—as it is, in numerous climaxes in which Pantaloon is cuckolded. Silent slapstick offered many sublimations, obvious and subtle, of the obscene and the sallacious. Though early slapstick was considered quite risque, Laurel and Hardy could do no more than gesture their desire to fondle a girl's private parts.

V. INTERLUDE: "THE VIRGIN OF VENICE"

Based on commedia dell'arte scenarios.
A *Playboy* Ribald Classic.
Retold by David Madden.

For three years, Leandro remained desperately faithful to Cintia. He had left Venice on a trading voyage to the Orient and his head had whirled as he walked through the bazaars seeing the lovely, miniature, supple Annamese girls all around him. Or the soft, brown women of Luzon; or the exotic, inviting girls of Cathay. Though his brow often broke out in sweat from the feverish itch he felt in other places, Leandro remained a virgin.

But all for nought. When he finally went back to Venice, his ship laden with silks and spices, he was greeted with the terrible news that Coviello, the rich merchant who employed him, had wooed and won not Cintia but her parents—who had prevailed on her to marry. Leandro arranged a meeting with her in order to pour out his bitterness.

Before he could begin, Cintia cried, "It was such a long time, my darling! And I kept imagining you in the arms of some Oriental

girl. Forgive me for my weakness—I am no more to be blamed than
a slave who was bought in the market. Coviello collects women as
he collects gold pieces—tonight he is after Pantalone's young wife,
Flaminia. So forgive me, my dear, and come to me tonight."

That evening, Leandro disguised himself as a beggar and made
his way through the dark streets toward Coviello's *palazzo*. But on
the way, he ran into old Pantalone's manservant, Zanni, who stopped
him, saying, "Listen, friend, I'll give you a sequin if you'll help me
carry this chest of lemons to the house of Pantalone. It's bloody
heavy." To avoid suspicion, Leandro agreed. After two steps, he
realized that the lemons were really a man and, in all probability,
the man was Coviello. When they loaded the chest into a gondola,
it was all Leandro could do to resist dropping it into the canal.

Flaminia herself, candle in hand, let them in through a back
door. They deposited the chest in the corridor and she said quickly,
"You are dismissed, Zanni, but I have some work for this other fellow." The door closed. The lovely Flaminia blew out her candle
and sighed, "Oh, darling Coviello, how clever of you to disguise
yourself as a beggar. I am burning for you, my dearest; take me here."
Leandro heard the swish of descending silks. He put out his hand and

met warm, round flesh. The young wife had laid her back on the lemon chest and was waiting.

Leandro was confused with revenge and desire. All he could think of were those three starved years while this pig of a Coviello was having his fill. Undoing his clothes, falling to his knees, Leandro lost in three minutes the virginity he had hoarded so long.

As he finished, there came an awful groan from the chest.

"What did you say?" asked Flaminia.

"I was merely expressing my sorrow that I must leave you. Pantalone will be home soon," Leandro whispered.

"Don't you remember? Franceschina agreed to tease him to-night. We have many hours. But let us spend them upstairs in a soft bed," Flaminia said. "Follow me soon, my dearest."

Leandro, however, did not follow. He tied some heavier knots in the rope around the chest, put on his clothes and his beggar's cloak and went into the street. It was not long before he almost ran into a man who was standing on a barrel, struggling awkwardly to get up onto a second-floor balcony.

"Beggar, give me a boost," the man said, and Leandro recognized Pantalone by his crooked frame and his bad breath.

Just as Pantalone had got halfway up, one leg and one arm hooked in the railings, the door of the house opened a crack and a sweet feminine voice whispered to Leandro, "Whatever are you doing out there, my darling Pantalone? Zanni won't be home—I worked up a thumping quarrel with him this morning. Do come in now." Leandro slipped inside, leaving the old man dangling.

The moonlight shone on a sweet face and a marvelous pair of _____. But Leandro could hardly believe what he saw. They looked too generous to be true. But Franceschina in an instant had pulled her robe about her, scampered up the stairs and had locked her door. The familiar fever struck Leandro's brain once again. The quick moment with Flaminia had not been enough to break the fast of three years. He bounded up the stairs and battered through the door. Luckily, his fall was broken by a soft female body. Leandro made the most of this coincidence.

"Oh, heavens!" Franceschina said, "You aren't Pantalone—you are . . . somebody else—mm—and a very strong, masterful somebody else—oh, mmm."

It was quite a long time—several times, in fact—before the fever left him and he began to remember that Cintia was waiting and that

he was already an hour late. He thought of Cintia's dear face; he
thought of her chestnut hair spread out on the pillow of a bed far
softer than this. So he gave Franceschina a final pinch in a charming place, dressed and stepped outdoors again.

Pantalone, exhausted and groaning, was still hanging from the
balcony. "Up you go, master," said Leandro, giving him a boost.
"The little lady is waiting for you." Then Leandro went down to
borrow a gondola. At the edge of the steps, he found the banished
Zanni asleep in his boat. He shook him by the shoulder. "Hurry,
friend, there is a thief getting into your house by the balcony," he
said. Zanni jumped up, seized his dagger and began to run.

Leandro himself had little trouble climbing the balcony of
Cintia's house. When he got to her room, he found her asleep, her
beautiful chestnut hair spread out on the pillow. "At last!" he
thought. "After three long years, I can have my love." But nothing
happened. He felt no fever, no sudden surge of passion, no desire
for his dearest Cintia. "I must have fallen out of love," he thought,
and a terrible weariness overcame him. He lay down on the bed and
fell asleep almost at once.

But thanks to the fact that Flaminia also slept a long and blissful sleep, thanks to the fact that Leandro's sailor knots were so stout that Coviello had, eventually, to be chopped out of the chest, thanks to the fact that Zanni was being hauled up before a magistrate for the murder of his master—thanks to all these things, Cintia and Leandro were undisturbed until noon. And when they awoke, they discovered that there are certain things that are just as voluptuous and exciting to do in the sunlight as in the dark.

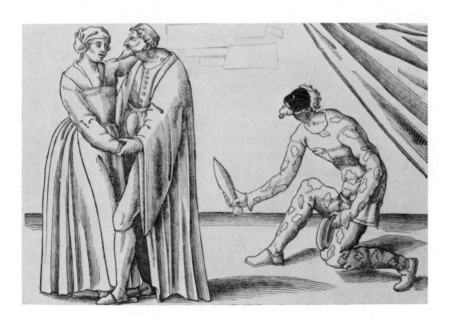

VI. IMPROVISATION

If the commedia actors were allowed to improvise almost at will, this freedom had its limitations in character. Each actor had a rich repertoire of set speeches and routine action that suited the character he portrayed. (In fact, it is one of Harlequin's traits as a character that he is always improvising upon situations; thus improvisation gives force to his personality.) The actors did not fill in the scenario outline with entirely extempore or impromptu routines. In both commedia and silent slapstick, skillful improvisation is the ability to make the right choice from a vast repertoire of learned speeches and antics precisely at the appropriate moment—in character.

When confronted with a blank moment in the action, improvise. Mabel Normand was directing a little comedy one day and wanted Chaplin to stand with a hose and water down the road so that the villain's car would skid, and Chaplin says, "I suggested standing on the hose so that the water can't come out, and when I look at the nozzle I unconsciously step off and get it in the face" (Chaplin, 148-49). In improvising to meet the needs of the moment, Chaplin reached for the very first slapstick gag recorded on film—twenty-five years earlier. Chaplin carried improvisation much further, into the realm of conception; mask and costume became inseparable from the function of the muse; he would order a set to be built, then stand fully costumed in the middle of the construction in progress, and wait for an idea that would fill the set with action.

Improvisation provides scope for individual inventiveness. But it is also in improvisation that the ensemble system of the commedia functions most creatively. Gradually, the Italians pushed this freedom so far into a traditional standardization that the ultimate result was a fully written script.

As the frontier pushed west, improvisation was a major trait in the American character. At each new frontier on toward the Pacific, the American asked, What next? His impulse was always to make it new. Thus, silent slapstick reflected the zanier side of this American character trait. In Italy and later in America, it was the natural function of improvisation to produce novelties.

When the form allows a basic freedom, the audience demands novelty, newness; when certain aspects are fixed, the actor can employ his imagination in discovering possibilities. And Harlequin and Charlie proved most imaginative, and improvised most audaciously when in the heat of danger. Spontaneity was another quality flowing naturally from improvisation.

The commedia spontaneously turned accidents on the stage or in the audience to advantage, and they built into their plays local legends or other contingencies as they roved from one town to an-

other. Both commedia and silent slapstick used local color quite
deftly. We see the raw new suburbs of Hollywood and Los Angeles
in the background of the films, and sometimes these are brought into
the foreground as Sennett loaded his camera crew and actors into
jalopies and raced to the scene of fires, floods, and parades, shot film,
and went back to the studio to build a story around the footage.

VII. *LAZZI* (SLAPSTICK) AND THE COMEDY OF FORCE

That aspect of improvisation which enabled the commedia to break out of its limitations most boisterously was, of course, the slapstick stage business—called *lazzi*, which means ribbon. The *lazzi*, like a ribbon, wound through the plot. The *lazzi* is a visual analysis of the logic of absurdity. Our term "slapstick" derives from Harlequin's bat, a stick made of two limber pieces of wood bound at the handle which made a very loud racket when applied vigorously to an exposed rump. It is the sudden bursts of *lazzi* that gives us in slapstick what André Bazin calls "that delicious vertigo" or Arthur Knight calls a "surreal," though "ordered insanity." In these bursts of *lazzi*, the participants enacted chaos seeking form, they exhibited form courting chaos.

There were two kinds of commedia—there was the trivial Neapolitan sort in which slapstick was an end in itself, diminishing the importance of character, and which flourished in southern Italy; Mack Sennett revived this type, though his parodies were on a slightly higher plane. Then there was the northern Italian commedia, subtler, wittier, in which laughter was provoked more by character revelation; Chaplin perfected this type.

Early commedia troupes rehearsed the scenario as such no more thoroughly than Sennett's people did: both groups might run briefly through the bare plot, trying to discover places for *lazzi*. Individuals might work out little *lazzi* routines separately with a partner. The problem was to avoid deviating so much from the basic plot with *lazzi* as to lose the thread and confuse the audience. The commedia constantly studied and practiced ancient comic business, but each day they were engaged in the actual execution of *lazzi* skills in public performance.

Lazzi was not just a matter of indiscriminately engaging in horseplay; these structured gags followed the logic of comedy with mathematical precision and the actors became masters of timing, pacing, and spacing, so that even when a routine familiar to the audience was brought into play, it came with a degree of surprise. Suspense was another element in some of the *lazzi*: the audience sees the cop or the captain with stick or sword in hand sneak up behind Charlie or Harlequin before the characters do.

Commedia and silent slapstick audiences loved to see human
and mechanical transformations. Thus in a commedia scenario, a
lovely fountain was discovered to be two men in disguise blowing
through tubes. In *Sherlock, Jr.*, Keaton, small-town movie projec-
tionist, dreams that he walks up into the movie being shown on the
screen; he dives into the sea, but the scene changes so that he lands
on hard rock. Camera tricks and editing and great imagination produced some awesome effects.

Slapstick is the comedy of force. In vengeance for a beating from his master, Harlequin often engineered a sequence of events which put Pantaloon through numerous beatings and violent accidents.

The savage encounters between man and man, and man and objects, in Laurel and Hardy movies especially, demonstrate the prevalence in the *lazzi* repertoire of violence and mayhem. In *Two Tars*, the genial pair demolish a car with their bare hands, and precipitate a chain of similar destruction down a long line of Sunday drivers. In *The Finishing Touch* they attempt to finish a house already half-way constructed and end up demolishing the entire sturcture.

Like the other verbal improvisational routines, many of the
lazzi had to be in character; thus the manager could instruct the
Harlequin actor at one point in the bare scenario to do a Harlequin
love *lazzi*, or fear, or jealousy, or rage, or menace *lazzi*.

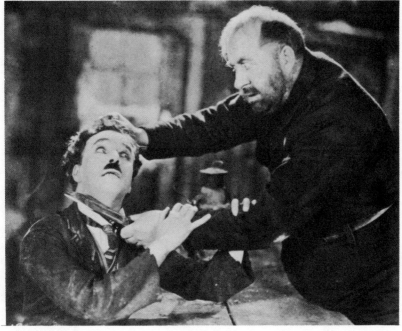

Lazzi familiar to us in silent slapstick were used in commedia—
the frantic-fright leap, obviously, the pratfall, various kicking routines.
The 108 (an acrobat's term for a comic fall involving a split and sudden backward somersault that lands the actor flat on his back, a feat
involving great risk and skill) was Ben Turpin's professional signa-
ture: he would often announce in public, "I'm Ben Turpin! $3000
a week!" and do a neat 108. The 108, like the salary, was who he
was. Holding a glass of wine, Tommaso Visentini, a great Harlequin,
could do a somersault without spilling a drop.

All these *lazzi* were, obviously, enhanced in the silent era by speeding up the camera or showing a sequence in reverse. The speed-up made the most of the chase especially, although Chaplin, a master of *lazzi*, deemphasized the chase, regarding it as a gratuitous wrap-up for the last reel.

"Little as I knew about movies, I knew that nothing transcended personality" (142).

Many of these *lazzi* were, of course, extremely dangerous, but the actors of both traditions were daredevils, though some daredevils were happily more skillful than others. Just as Harold Lloyd, with three fingers missing on one hand, has left us a record of the typical daredevil antic in *Safety Last*—in which he hangs from a window ledge and a clock hand on a tall building—we know that one Harlequin was famous for his own human fly act around the face of the auditorium.

The *lazzi* often involved the use of objects that were hazardous to the character and to the actor as well. The play of dangerous objects began with Harlequin's stick and Chaplin's cane—magic wands with which they ward off the evil spirits inhabiting other objects. Charlie's repetitious movements, which enable him either to adapt or escape, are camouflage imitations of the machines that threaten him everywhere he turns. "I am confident," says Bazin, "that in all Charlie's pictures there is not one where this mechanical movement does not end badly for him. In other words, mechanization of movement is in a sense Charlie's original sin, the ceaseless temptation" (151). Thus Harlequin's pure, comic mechanical movements became in our age of hostile technology both more comic and more frighteningly meaningful.

On the narrow commedia stages fewer machines or objects
afflicted Harlequin, but later in the new gigantic public theatres
whole towns were constructed and many stage machines employed.
Often the proper use of these objects and machines failed to serve
Harlequin and Charlie as they served other people; but the ingenuity
of Charlie and Harlequin enabled them to solve immediate problems
by forcing these objects into momentarily alien uses as when Charlie
uses a lamp post to subdue a bully (Bazin, 146). In silent films,
flivvers, streetcars, trains, were frequently demolished in use. Tread-
mills, revolving doors, vats of water were often used.

The scenes for commedia and silent slapstick were set in places calculated to produce machines and objects as levers for *lazzi*. The apothecary provided the Doctor with a stock *lazzi* prop—the enormous enema syringe; drawings show posteriors bared to receive the enema, which sometimes splashes an old woman's face. Silent slapstick exploited barber shops, laundries, hotel lobbies, kitchens, factories, beauty parlors, movie theatres, and film studios.

The bakery shop provided Mabel Normand in 1913 with a pie.
Ben Turpin's cross-eyes were failing to spark a laugh as he stuck his
head in a doorway. Improvised *lazzi* to the rescue. Mabel, sitting on
the sidelines, noticed a workman's lunch pie. "Motion picture history," says Mack Sennett, "millions of dollars, and a million laughs
hung on her aim as the custard wabbled in a true curve and splashed
with a dull explosion in Ben Turpin's face." Like the spitting routines
of Harlequin, pie-throwing became such "a distinguished facet of
cineplastic art" that a special throwing pie was invented. Berry pies
were preferred but creams had their justifications. Thousands of pies
later, in Laurel and Hardy's *The Battle of the Century*, 1,500 pies
were thrown in one day. Like slipping on a banana peel, the pie in
the face is an elementary *lazzi* for the downfall of authority or false
dignity. "It represents," says Sennett, "a fine, wish-filling, universal
idea, especially in the face of authority, as in the cop or mother-in-
law situation."[10]

Animals were often good for a *lazzi* in both commedia and silent slapstick: donkeys, horses, monkeys, lions, bears, giraffes, turkeys, dogs, goats, skunks, elephants, etc. In addition to animals, or in lethal conjunction with them, kids—brats, that is—were often employed, though more frequently in silent films.

A favorite target of *lazzi* was the body, with preference given to the posterior—which accidentally encountered a hot surface or a finger, or the Captain's or Pantaloon's sword. The skull, the nose, the ears, the back, the hands, the toes were often targets of a wide range of somatic gags. Bare breasts and bare buttocks and false phalluses contributed to the bawdiness, the lasciviousness (as some Victorian commentators eagerly pointed out) of these gags. The pulling-of-teeth routine aroused empathy and laughter simultaneously in the audience.

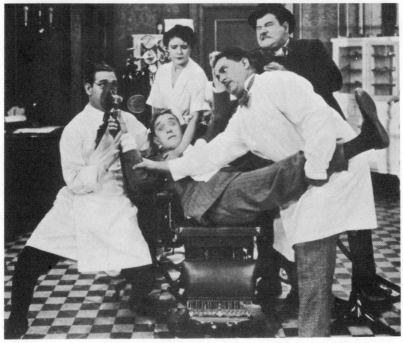

Many *lazzi* made use of basic human necessities such as food. Harlequin's frequent attempts to satisfy his gluttony (often depicted in paintings and drawings) are reversed in Charlie's pathetic effort to wring some nourishment from his boiled shoe in *Gold Rush*. Drunkenness quite obviously provides many opportunities for *lazzi*. Then, what one eats and drinks, must be evacuated, and there is a category of *lazzi* to take care of that necessary function.

But both commedia and silent slapstick provided subtle *lazzi*
as well. If we want to imagine Harlequin's gentler *lazzi*, we have
only to recall the nuances Chaplin gave to many stock bits of comic
business, as for instance his brushing aside gesture—in "The Adven-
turer," he escapes from prison, is crawling around, encounters the
warden's shoe, and kicks a little snad over it with his hand. Hardy
was a master of gesture *lazzi*—the tie-twiddle used to mollify a bully
or a girl, his baroque way of signing his name, his you-after-me
routine with Laurel that always leads to a more violent *lazzi*.

Despite the prevalence of *lazzi* and frantic activity, a certain
naturalness is often ascribed to the commedia style of acting. Frantic
movement itself was natural enough in their everyday lives as they
fled one city after another, eluding civil and ecclesiastical wrath.
Silent slapstick comedians also, of course, came out of a tradition of
theatrical roving in vaudeville and burlesque.

The ability to make judicious use of *lazzi* was a major skill of
the professional comedy actor. Overzealous surrender to the vertigo
of *lazzi* often collapsed into pointless farce. Commedia and Keystone
comedy at their worst were 90 percent *lazzi*. This characterless farce
encourages, of course, the use of grotesques, so that we find hunch-

backs and dwarfs in decadent commedia, and Sennett himself inclined to over-populate his lot with actual or fabricated grotesques. The ultimate success of *lazzi* depended upon the ability of the actors to play together, and many fine actors were plagued by partners who were inept at *lazzi*.

VIII. STAGE AND CAMERA: TRIUMPH THROUGH LIMITATIONS

The stages and theatres of commedia and silent slapstick imposed limitations upon the actors which forced them to develop skills that not only compensated for those limitations but transcended them. On the small, tight trestle stages, the commedia actors had to develop techniques of economy which necessitated a certain stylization of movement while conveying the illusion of a ranging freedom; these stylized movements survived the cramped conditions in which they evolved. When they moved into new, spacious public theatres such as the Palladio in Vicenza this economy of movement was retained but spread out over a larger canvass.

The Art Institute of Chicago

And the silent slapstick comics brought similar economic movements and gestures with them from the various kinds of theatres in which they were trained. The early movie studios, with their cramped sets, created traffic problems that encouraged the actors to retain their theatrical movements, so that when they began to race around Hollywood and Los Angeles we experienced delightful tension between landscape space and tight bodily movements.

In the early days of the commedia, a troupe might play on a trestle stage at a crossroads one day and at a king's palace the next. Silent slapstick history shows a somewhat similar contrast, though the time factor differs—from tent or barnlike theatres to the fabulous movie palaces. In such towns as Venice, as many as six plays might be presented on platform stages in the same piazza at the same time just as Keaton, Chaplin, and Lloyd might appear on different screens on the same day in Chicago. The backgrounds added a certain strange aura—as life went on normally in the piazzas. And on the film itself normal life went on in the raw suburbs of southern California in the background while the crazy antics progressed in the foreground. The small trestle stage and the small silver screen had this in common: they made talent or lack of it highly visible.

On the small studio stages as well as on the platform commedia
stages, scenery was sketchy, flimsy, and there was room for few
elaborate machines or props. But in the large public theatres of
Italy, where opera was the other most popular theatrical mode, the
sets were spectacularly sturdy and somewhat realistic, with streets
in perspective. In the same silent movie, Chaplin might move out of
an obvious studio set into the realistic milieu of the streets.

Simplicity of scenery for the commedia was also dictated by
the economics of constant travel; consequently, the commedia
showed succeeding eras what could be accomplished with set and
prop limitations. Silent slapstick contrasts with commedia in this
respect: "Slapstick made a protagonist out of space" (Bazin, 121).
Before montage, "most of its gags derived from a comedy of space."

In early silent slapstick, the immobility of the camera and the
fixedness of the studio stage constituted a limitation—to be unable
to speak is one thing, to be confined in movement is too restrictive.
So when the camera began to move about, a new freedom added
another dimension to basic slapstick elements—space. Camera place-
ment, said Chaplin, is "cinematic inflection," it "was not only psy-
chological but articulated a scene" (151). "My own camera setup

is based on facilitating choreography for the actor's movements.
. . . The camera should not obtrude" (255). Griffith and others
taught the slapstick camera how to plant gags with selective close-
ups. Commedia actors had other ways of focusing; special use of
the body was one; and of course, silent slapstick also used the body
as a means of creating montage within a frame (a technique cur-
rently heralded as new).

Through trick photography and special editing effects, silent
slapstick could, of course, achieve effects no commedia troupe ever
dreamed of. Pies appeared to swing around telephone poles in pur-
suit of their targets. But the camera and film editors could also
ruin some fine moments. Chaplin had to contend with machines
and mechanical minds off screen as well as on: "The butchers in
the cutting room. Familiar with their method of cutting films, I
would contrive business and gags just for entering and exiting from
a scene, knowing that they would have difficulty in cutting them
out" (148).

The camera was also capable of making certain *lazzi* appear
less mechanical. Charlie is leaning over a ship rail, appearing to be
seasick. From another camera angle, however, we see that he is only

fishing. On the commedia stage, Harlequin would have to turn
around to cinch the gag. Some effects are possible only with the
collaboration of the camera: Charlie Murry is tied to a boiler which
begins to expand, then an exterior shot shows the whole house ex-
panding.

IX. SOUND AND SILENCE

In silent slapstick the major limitation was, of course, imposed externally— a technological limitation: absence of sound. The very term slapstick refers, ironically, to the sound produced by a slapstick in the noisiest part of the commedia production. But in a sense, even in commedia, the sound itself was not important so much as the impression of physical pain amplified by the sound. This is a synesthesic technique—just as certain sounds induce the sight of a color. So that through the sensory phenomenon of synesthesia we might say that a kind of visual sound was produced in silent slapstick. The cacophony of mass destruction in Laurel and Hardy's *Big Business* or *Two Tars* is *heard*, whether seen in a large theatre where sound effects sometimes accompanied the films or in the small-town theatres where the silent sound was seen more clearly.

In *Leave 'Em Laughing*, Laurel and Hardy were given too much laughing gas at the dentist's. The spectacle of the boys simply laughing, while also reacting to pain, is contagious, so that the audience, which hears no laughter, laughs until it gags at the mere *sight* of prolonged laughter. (A wildly popular recording years before, consisting of nothing but laughter, variously modulated, had a similar effect.) Another synesthetic effect was the sight of a pie in the kisser, which produced in the imagination's ear a sound—"splurch." Silent slapstick transcended its limitation of silence with many other ingenious compensations.

Instrumental music and singing enlivened the commedia productions, and usually music accompanied silent slapstick if only on a tinny piano. The demonic Brighella, who could lapse into lyrical guitar playing, is resurrected with the advent of sound in Harpo at his harp, Chico at his piano.

Actual sound effects accompanying the *lazzi* are only one element that is missing—silent movies did not speak. Synesthesia is
little help here. The use of titles to provide key lines of dialogue,
vital narrative information, and comment on the action never made
anyone happy. Since commedia actors could speak, dialogue was
extremely important, but like the early *sound* slapstick movies, the
commedia plays often talked too much, and when one looks at some
of the scenarios which do include written dialogue, one observes that
much of it is pretty tedious—like the unfunny translations of Molière.
But this literary element—whether written in or employed improvisa-
tionally from the actor's repertoire of learned set speeches—was
always secondary to the action in commedia. Just as we enjoy
Groucho's insane gibberish, we're glad when he shuts up and the
three brothers plunge into action. Without the inflections of the
voice, the silent slapstick actor must develop all the more his talent
for communicating emotion through gestures, through his body.

    For the many rhetorical devices used in commedia dialogue,
silent slapstick found visual equivalents. If a commedia scene often
ended on a rhetorical flourish, Charlie simply rounded a corner in his
peculiar way—fade out. If audiences enjoyed listening to Pantaloon

extend a metaphor, film audiences enjoyed the visual analysis of a gage premise as in the ice cream sequence in the Edgar Kennedy short "A Pair of Tights."

The nature of the commedia allowed the actors to speak, but they often became enslaved to this freedom, while one might say that the machine freed them in their film reincarnation by imposing upon them the limitation of silence.

X. PLAYING THE MASK

The major conventional limitation with which commedia was blessed
was the use of masks for the five major stock characters. But Goldoni
wasn't much interested in limitations; he was a freedom lover. If the
masks make it difficult to convey emotions, eliminate the masks:
"The mask," he said, "must always be very prejudicial to the action
of the performer either in joy or sorrow; whether he be in love, cross,
or good-humored, the same features are always exhibited; and however he may gesticulate and vary the tone, he can never convey by
the countenance, which is the interpreter of the heart, the different
passions with which he is inwardly agitated. . . . The actor must,
in our days, possess a soul; and the sould under a mask is like fire
under ashes."[11]

David Garrick expressed a counter attitude; when he revived
John Rich's *Harlequin's Invasion*, playing it without a mask, he
added a prologue tribute to Rich (known as Lun):

> When Lun appear'd, with matchless art and whim
> He gave the pow'r of speech to every limb;
> Tho' mask'd and mute, conveyed his quick intent,
> And told in frolic gestures all he meant.

Behind this limitation a powerful blessing is latent. With his
own face hidden, the actor playing Harlequin, for instance, is forced
to project his character's emotions with his body. His gestures must
speak. In the slight margin between fixity and flux, he must shape
the nuances of his *own* Harlequin. Though Harlequin's face never
changes, his body speaks differently every moment, in every play.
Though Harlequin's face remains neutral, it is full of possibilities
which his body and his voice articulate.

The commedia actors spoke of the skill of playing the mask—
with it and against it. The inanimate mask and the animate body
enhance each other. The commedia also used the voice, of course.
Silent slapstick had only the body, but the actor's masks were only
semi- or modified masks, made up of Chaplin's, Hardy's, and the
Keystone Kops' mustaches, Lloyd's glasses, Chaplin's made-up eye-
brows, Hardy's bangs with the spit curls, and Stan's slit eyes (resem-
bling Harlequin's).

The actor's own God-given features were exploited, too: Turpin's crossed eyes, Langdon's baby face.

Chaplin gives us some impression of the effect of the mask (which may include an inseparable costume), upon the wearer: "With the clothes on I felt that day on the Keystone lot, that the Tramp was a reality, a living person. In fact, he ignited all sorts of crazy ideas that I would never have dreamt of, until I was dressed and made up as the Tramp" (147). Keaton's great stone face is so close to being a mask that some commentators are encouraged to make deeper philosophical, metaphysical interpretations of the significance of his face in particular and of masks in general. Lloyd's comment is simple, but adequate: "By not smiling, Buster made his task all the more difficult. Like all good comics his body movements were generally funny. But he had to depend on his body and go along on that same facial expression." [12]

Even the soft leather masks of the commedia had a certain mobility, the masks of the silent slapstick actors were much more mobile: Charlie's smile and the curl he gave his lip, lifting that tuft of mustache; Stan Laurel's slow cry and his scratch, raising his hair in a stiff thatch; Hardy's famous stare or camera-look; Edgar Kennedy's slow burn; Finlayson's double-take and fade away—all these expressions are fixtures of the mobile, portmanteau mask.

The five commedia masks were made more effective and expressive by juxtaposition to the characters who *didn't* wear masks. This value operated in silent slapstick as well; the girls in both commedia and silent slapstick were there for their beauty, adorned only by cosmetics and costumes.

The mask the actor plays is his dominant theatrical image; it is the outward manifestation of the soul of the character. John Grierson remarked sadly in 1932 that "masks, the greatest of all the gifts of the Silent comedy, are become mere faces again."[13] But it was not just their distinctive masks that set commedia and silent slapstick characters off and made them poetic, iconographical images, but masks and costumes, together with the typical bodily stances.

XI. THE BODY: A LANGUAGE OF GESTURES

With either the face covered or the voice muted, the body had to supplement those limitations. The use of the body was itself limited at times in Renaissance Italy when the commedia played the narrow, trestle stages in the piazzas. This reliance upon the body to do the work of the face or the voice necessitated the cultivation of the art of pantomime or mimicry.

The commedia actors spoke a language of gestures. They sculpted life in motion on the air. The art of the gesture extended from expressive poses and postures to the most exacting gymnastics. Looking at silent slapstick stunts we get some sense of the commedia actor's acrobatic skill in feats of running, leaping, falling, and tumbling. Harlequin's incredible acrobatic skill made his imbalances all the more ridiculously funny.

120

The stances of the various characters became so stylized that the body too became a mask. One might speak of "playing the back." Harlequin could make himself taller or shorter, and he had distinctive mannerisms involving the use of his slapstick and the handling of his hat. His unique walk also reminds us of Charlie. Harlequin's was an impertinent, arrogant, self-mocking stiff-legged, flatfooted strut. The oddball walk is, of course, a characteristic of Buster Keaton, Stan Laurel, Harry Langdon, and Groucho Marx. Scaramouche, at 80, could box a man's ears with his feet. Bazin called Chaplin's backward kick, capable of conveying many character attitudes and nuances, a "vital approach" to life with many meanings (150).

Another major use of the body in commedia was the dance. In contrast to the learned comedy, with its intermezzi or interludes, commedia often laced the play itself with dancing and music; its ballerinas were a great attraction. The influence of ballet in Chaplin's movements had often been remarked (see "The Rink" and "The Floor-walker," for instance). And, of course, the Keystone comedy generally exhibited in its chases the choreography of chaos. The mixing of slapstick with song and dance was characteristic of many Laurel and Hardy and other comedy team movies in the early era of sound.

XII. PLAYING THE COSTUME

Stylization of masks, movements, and costumes was a limitation, but each enabled the other to transcend limitations in a controlled manner. If we can speak of playing the mask and of playing the body, we can also speak of playing with or against the stock costume.

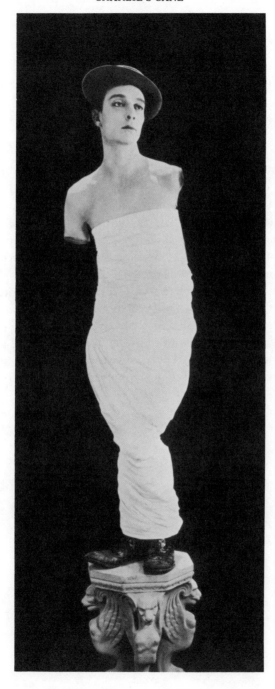

Costumes enhanced contrasts between age and youth, ugliness
and beauty, dignity and foolishness. The lovers dressed like the
fashionable young people in the audience. But the *zannis* dressed in
sloppy clothes, or tight clothes, or tight but many-colored outfits.
Each mask character wore a distinctive hat. We see combinations of
these costume items in the silent comedians. Harlequin's heelless
shoes and Pantaloon's Turkish-style slippers are famous, but Charlie's,
Harry's, and Keaton's oversize shoes were used even more consciously.
Of course, in silent films we miss the color that was characteristic of
commedia costumes and masks. Both commedia and silent slapstick
make wonderful use of costumes in the various disguise plots. In one
of these Harlequin is dressed half as a woman, half as a man; and
most of the commedia and silent comics enjoyed dressing up as
women.

They also enjoyed acting out role reversals, as when Harlequin literally became a mother, and Laurel and Hardy or Chaplin were forced into house-wifely chores.

XIII. ORIGINS IN THE MARKET PLACE

One arm of the commedia tradition is Al Capp's comic strip which, as the cartoonist himself says, is based, like all comedy, on "man's inhumanity to man." We see this inhumanity in its purest form in that frightening Laurel and Hardy movie *Big Business*, in which Finlayson destroys the boys' car while they demolish his house—in a prophetic parody of the riots of the sixties. But comedy is also "a healthy deflation of man's dangerous pretenses and pompous self-deception." Capp goes on to say that comedy can become sublime "when it makes men sorrow at man's inhumanity to man by making men pity themselves," as in certain Chaplin films.[14] Chaplin himself says: "Through humor, we see in what seems rational, the irrational; in what seems important, the unimportant. It also heightens our sense of survival and preserves our sanity" (211).

If Bazin is correct in saying that "laughter allows the audience to become aware of itself" (121), perhaps he is more aware than the audience that the impact of public approval gives birth to comic characters and that the public collaborates with actors in the evolution of those characters. It is the public which hands down to succeeding generations timeless, changeless masks. The commedia is a popular comedy, irresistible to the people because the people were irresistible to the actors. The public was their livelihood, their mentor, their god. They didn't go to the tombs of the Greeks—they let the courtiers perpetuate on paper their thin effusions—but to the marketplace for their inspirations.

The theatre being offered in Italy just before 1550 was mainly amateur farce and religious plays. (In supplanting the religious theatre, the commedia dell'arte provoked the scorn of the church and was forced to submit to its control.) The learned comedies of the academies, like the American theatre of the 1910's and 1920's, was confined to large towns and special audiences. The commedia dell'arte itself derived from the satyr plays and New Comedy of the classical Greek theatre, from Roman popular comedy, from the tumblers, jugglers, conjureres, tightrope dancers, clowns, mountebank

quacks, the exiled Byzantine mimes, and the strolling players of the
Middle Ages, who showed up at fairs and carnivals. These strolling
fugitives offered a continually changing ensemble of characters.
Centuries of improvisation freed shadowy character types from their
substances and made the shadows larger than life.

"Comedy that is basic will live forever," says Harold Lloyd, because its language is universal (Cahn, 20). Both commedia and silent slapstick were grand new flowerings of basic popular entertainment elements that had always existed before, continued to exist alongside of, and *after* each of these. But as André Bazin points out, the classical commedia style of farce seemed to have atrophied since the eighteenth century; but it had "a sudden and dazzling rebirth" in silent slapstick in what was a "spontaneous linking up of a genre with its Tradition" (150). Two things made that spontaneity possible: a technological invention—cinema itself—and a sociological responsiveness to the possibilities of that invention. The characteristic we experience most intensely about these two comic media is their youthfulness, and it is in their early phases that they are most interesting and comparable to each other.

American silent slapstick derived from popular entertainment forms that had kept vital commedia dell'arte routines, formulas, plots, characters, costumes, and masks alive: Harlequin lifts his hat, Charlie his cane, and the dead rascals of centuries become quick. Though he made the obvious Chaplin comparison, Ducharte, one of the best commentators on commedia, observed in 1929 that its last vestiges were to be seen in the marionette shows (120). Chaplin and other slapstick comics saw Punch and Judy, too.

While most of the commedia actors were trained *in* the commedia troupes themselves, most of the silent slapstick actors came from the ranks of the American minstrel shows, the circus clowns, the stage comics of the Victoria London Music Hall, the rubes and buffoons of vaudeville and burlesque. In the theatre of the Victorian era (our own Dark Ages for the theatre), "once stage business had been tried out and set," says Chaplin, "one rarely attempted to invent new business" (153). These rigid routines were given new freedom in silent slapstick.

The influence of foreign movies was decisive. Early slapstick movies were born in a thirty-second burst of water from a garden hose on the Lumiere Brothers' lot in 1895. By 1907, the chase was on, with Cohl's *The Pumpkin Race.*

Chaplin studied the style of Max Linder, an elegant man who wore a tiny mustache and a derby and carried a cane, and who as early as 1905 appeared in a Zecca farce in the commedia tradition: *La Vie de Polcchinelle*. Sennett tells us that he tried the "dizzying camera tricks he admired in French chases" (Knight, 41). So what had proven most vital in French, Italian, Jewish, and English comic traditions was yoked violently to the enormous energy of a youthful nation grasping for its own folk art.

XIV. WANDERING TROUPES AND LAUGH FACTORIES

As regards acting companies, commedia and silent slapstick are quite similar in many ways. The commedia actor-manager was also the director (a Leo McCarey—Hal Roach combination). A commedia company consisted of about thirteen actors; but that many recognizable faces composed only the nucleus of Keystone. The commedia troupes moved around from town to town; the slapstick laugh factories were fixed, but their films circulated all over the world. So did its material and its actors, as Keystone, Vitagraph, Biograph, United Artists stole gags and lured actors from each other. Some significant comparisons and contrasts between commedia and silent slapstick arise when we compare Francesco Andrieini's Gelosi company (1570 to about 1604) with Sennett's University of Nonsense in Edendale. The various commedia companies had expressive names: The Confidenti, the Uniti, the Accesi (Inspired), the Desiosi (Desirous), the Fedeli (Faithful).

Both commedia and silent films (as in Chaplin's mocking impersonation of Hitler) pushed pure slapstick into satire. Just as commedia offered popular adaptations and parodies of classic "high art" and travesties of the learned comedy (itself based on Plautus and Terrance), silent slapstick offered parodies of "serious" movies (Stan Laurel's *Mud and Sand*) or of works in other media such as opera (Chaplin's *Carmen*). But in the work of both Gozzi in eighteenth-century Italy and Chaplin in America we see that topical satire can dull the impact of more basic and universal comic elements.

In both commedia and silent slapstick there was a great deal of mixing of different genres: satire and parody, obviously; the pastorale (more of this in Chaplin's than in any other slapstick comedy); the melodrama (less in commedia than in silent slapstick, where its features often scowl). If slapstick is often pushed beyond farce and satire to the absurd, there is also a mixing of the comic and the tragic. But whereas commedia troupes could perform a straight comedy one night and a pure tragedy the next, silent slapstick films had to blend the two genres very carefully. Early, Chaplin learned from a spectator on the set that he had the "ability to evoke tears as well as laughter" (153). Thus were the tragic postures of his childhood transformed into comic gestures. But except for Buster Keaton, the major slapstick comics (Chaplin, Langdon, Lloyd) lunged at pathos—and often collapsed into Victorian sentimentality.

Since commedia plays derived their elements from every possible source, the main source, in time, became other commedia plays. And silent slapstick is one vast reservoir of comic routines that have been practically in the public domain since ancient times; so silent movies only *appear* to plagiarize from each other. Both commedia and silent slapstick have taken transfusions from every conceivable high and low culture literary and theatrical antecedent for their life's blood.

Ironically, both have survived their major competitors: the non-commedia drama in Italy was of no lasting importance; little American theatre of the period of slapstick cinema's reign has survived; and although some of the "serious" movies (*Sunrise*) are dear to students of the film, few can be enjoyed by the throngs who even today find silent slapstick awesomely zany.

But there were of course, always, many dull, bad commedia troupes, as there were many tedious Sennett farces. Commedia was potent for two hundred years, but had become repetitious, vulgar, inept, grossly farcical, and decadent after 1750 and was dead by 1800. Silent slapstick's golden age was much briefer (1903 to about 1927); since new actors could not perpetuate its characters, it died in one stroke—the invention that gave it birth devoured it in one of its major

improvements: sound. Paradoxically, when the slapstick was heard, it lost its power. Such artistic reforms as Goldoni's—he wanted to abolish the masks and flesh out the skeletonal scenarios—precipitated the commedia's decline. And while his own artistic aspirations may have helped ruin Chaplin, a technological improvement that would enable the slapstick to be heard was the major cause of silent comedy's suicide.

Commedia influenced Goldoni, Lope de Vega, Molière, and Shakespeare, and, through silent slapstick, its verve and its more profound implications are seen in Beckett's *Waiting for Godot* and other absurd and black comedy plays, and in the films of Godard, de Broca, Jacques Tati, Peter Sellers, and Lester. The commedia characters are seen in their own guise in Carne's *Children of Paradise*, and in three films that appeared in 1952: Chaplin's *Limelight*—the ballet sequence, "The Death of Columbine"; Renoir's *The Golden Coach*, with Anna Magnani as Columbine; and MGM's *Scaramouche*.[15]

XV. LIMITATIONS (2)

At every point in a comparison of commedia dell'arte and silent
slapstick, we find forceful substantiation of a basic aesthetic principle: that the source of genius is an ability to control externally imposed limitations and a recognition of the necessity to risk imposing
certain limitations upon oneself in order to realize one's potential.
The actor must subordinate himself to the demands of his fellow
actors, while giving his own abilities full scope and thrust. Since his
character was set, his only freedom is in his art. His task is to control
that freedom.

We see this principal at work even in the amorphous, rowdy,
self-indulgent audience, which helps create, and then insists on the
observance of, certain confining conventions; but within these conventions, the spectator's imagination is encouraged to range and soar.
Because of the film medium's greater visual realism, the moviegoer
participates more easily but less imaginatively.

XVI. ACTORS AND AUDIENCES COLLABORATE

Actors and audiences participate in a metaphysical conspiracy against mortality to raise the stock and the standard to the level of art. They sometimes—as in Harlequin and Chaplin—succeed. There is a wisdom in the popular taste that the masses have always felt and sophisticates have always later discovered. Intellectuals do not discover that some things are avant-garde until after the masses have discarded them. When Harlequin's titanic energy overflowed the public squares into the palaces, his antics became high art for those aristocratic snobs who had once scorned his origins among the serfs. It took a Canadian intellectual to trumpet what was obvious to the Greeks and Italians and to America's melting-pot multitudes in the 1910's and 1920's—that the "medium is the massage."

We search the libraries in vain for the *early* commedia plays. Free of playwrights, the commedia actors imitated themselves, and fixed, not on paper, but in their costumes and masks, immortal characters. Outside the law, outside the church, they were alive in the laughter of the people—and that laughter was their religion and their law.

I once wrote of Chaplin: "The tramp's success as an everyman figure depends upon there being no man behind the mask, for he is, in a profound sense, a creature of the folk imagination. He underwent a slow realization and articulation, and, giving him his cues, international audiences collaborated in the process."[16] Chaplin did not premeditate the Tramp; he discovered him in the same way the comedies were once made: on the fly, almost by accident. The shape of the figure and his acts were one, perceived profoundly, responded to thoroughly in an instant. Chaplin often looked at his films with his audience: "The stir and excitement at the announcement of a Keystone Comedy, those joyful little screams that my first appearance evoked even before I had done anything, were most gratifying" (152).

One night in Rome, Goldoni sat in the audience for the premiere of one of his new plays; when Punch did not appear in the play, the uproar in the pit was so frightening that the playwright left early (Nagler, 280-81). Keaton had a similar experience: "I tried smiling at the end of one picture. The preview audience hated it and hooted the scene. . . . I never smiled again" (Cahn, p. 65). Audiences force comic characters into existence and certain actors into stylization out of a childlike insistence: "Do it again! The *same* way."

The commedia's success lay in its ability to get the feel of its audience and then to play directly to it; silent slapstick comics had a small, jaded, studio audience, and often visited the movie houses—as Stan Laurel did to clock laughs—but they seldom played directly to the camera, since it was only an abstract proxy for an audience. Sennett had one advantage over the commedia: if a gag misfired, he could always reshoot it, whereas the commedia could only employ one of many cover techniques. By taking its materials from all classes and playing to them, the commedia was a genuinely popular comedy; silent slapstick, however, aimed more directly at the lower and middle classes which identified with the little-guy-underdog figure. In both cases, each member of the audience was made to feel superior to his prototype on stage or screen.

Audiences collaborate with actors not only in creating characters, but also in creating the stars who portray those characters. The commedia was an ensemble of actors and characters, but audiences insisted on choosing their favorites, and their choices differed from region to region and era to era. Of course, even with the American star system—forced upon the industry by audience preferences—a

different sort of ensemble playing was achieved. Communications
media make stars: rumor, mostly, made them in Renaissance Italy;
the mass media, working faster and more decisively, made them in
modern America. If the affection of the masses can make godlike
stars—more, ironically, in a democracy than in feudal Italy—the
admiring scrutiny of sophisticates can break stars (as in the case of
Langdon who took them too seriously). The most brutal test of
comedy is its export power, and both commedia and American silent
slapstick passed that test by speaking so strongly in the universal
language of comic pantomime that their popularity exceeded that
of the native comedy with which they competed. The invocation
for this universal language made flesh is "Do it again!" Surprise is
not, as Bazin observes, as important as the anticipation and recognition of perfection (148).

   The audience makes the most important contribution to the
evolution of a character, for an actor can only introduce a character
—it is the audience who accepts or rejects him. The Italian audiences
no doubt behaved as the silent cinema audiences did when they re-
jected Harold Lloyd's Lonesome Luke in favor of his all-American
zany optimist. The audience encourages or disapproves of the gradual

stylizations of the character's image, as we see in the iconographic depiction of the evolution of Harlequin's costume from colored patches to formal diamonds.

Ultimately revelations of comic character are more endearing to an audience and to the actor than gags. Neither is interested mainly in the thing being done, but in who is doing it. The basic traits of the character are set, but it is within those limitations of character that the actor exercises his talent and the audience its admiration to the full. As many different actors portrayed Harlequin in 300 years, certain variations emerged; but the same actor played the Tramp, though Chaplin put him through many variations, and many comedians had a go at Charlie-like characters.

Each actor in the commedia perfected a single role over a lifetime, sometimes created a significant variation, and in many instances passed it on to his son. It was an actor-centered theatre in which the actor had to be a playwright in the heat and flash of the performance itself. And more than any other film genre, silent slapstick was actor-centered. Both types permitted the triumph of the actor as sheer creator.

Audiences were able to see their creations grow, because new facets were always accumulating to the stock figures, and this process of growth, accelerated in the films, lent the characters a sort of three-dimensional quality. This quality was achieved also in the techniques for playing against one's own type and with or against one's opposite (Harlequin and Pantaloon, Charlie and Mack Swain); the mocking mimicry of one's opposite was always a mode of self-definition. One could also play with or against one's partner—Harlequin and Brid-hella or Laurel and Hardy.

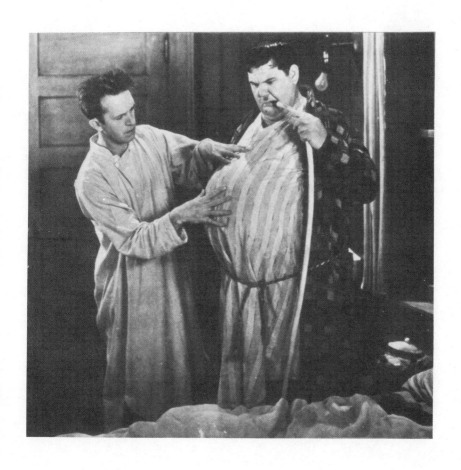

Silent slapstick offered a plethora of series films based on its
stars, while commedia was one series only, perpetuated over centuries,
with an antecedent in the Atellan Roman character Maccus.

In the old world, anything fresh and vigorous would naturally
incline toward artificiality, seeking a tradition in which to perpetuate
itself; silent slapstick was still inventive when it became a technological casualty, but the nature of its presentation—shadows, virtual
images—was artificial. Both the artificial commedia conventions
and the artificial slapstick medium of presentation evoked auras of
a strange and special kind of reality.

One major source of realism that was always active behind the
character facade was the real lives of the actors themselves. Commedia actors leave more testimony about money problems, daily
hardships. competition with rival companies, jealousies within troupes
—caused mainly by the presence of actresses—than about the intri-
cacies of their art. But they tended to confuse their real lives with
the behavior of the characters they played; like the Hollywood
comics, many of them came to bad ends; many played themselves
on stage, as Harry Langdon played himself on the screen. More in-
directly, Chaplin, as a person, it seems to me, is "a man of many

masks; most of them out of the rag-bag of the commedia dell'arte:
the lover, the pretentious Doctor and the sententious Pantaloon (as
in parts of his autobiography: he was 70 when he began it . . .); a
little of the braggart, El Capitano; Harlequin above all, in the Tramp,
who sometimes merges with the malicious Brighella; and he ultimately
arrives at Monsieur Verdoux's weary cynicism. Intentionally and
unintentionally, he shows himself to be vain, pompous, opinionated,
spiteful, and greedy. But he is also impulsively kind, sympathetic,
and thoughtful. In recounting incidents of his life-long shyness he
is charming" (FQ, 57-58). If Chaplin was greedy, it was pride in
quality and delight in making people laugh that generated the energy
which earned him his wealth.

CONCLUSION: "JE RENAIS"

Commedia and silent slapstick were the most unique theatrical and cinematic achievements of their times. The best commedia lasted 100 years, the best slapstick about 20 (the modern equivalent of about 150 years). Both were the most commercial of their time, but also without trying to be, both were classic folk arts and their works were artistic achievements.

The commedia has survived as sketchy scenarios—and in the silent slapstick films themselves. These films show both the essence of commedia and the manifold exfoliations of its rejuvenation in silent slapstick. Attempts to revive commedia in its purity or in some adulterated form usually prove dreary. Silent slapstick fares better—but, for the general public, mainly as a novelty and a curiosity. Whether or not we prefer commedia and silent slapstick over current comic modes, we *have* the comedy that is right for *us*—like it or not.

Both are gone—and though we feel a great sense of loss, neither can be willed back to life. *However*, the ashes of the phoenix still smolder. When the Italian comedy made its triumphant return to the Hotel de Bourgogne in Paris in 1697, "Je Renais" and a phoenix emblem were painted on the curtain. Sennett himself might have used such a motto. It would be interesting to discover whether Sennett ever heard of the commedia dell'arte.

Let the manager in *Fugitive Masks* have the last word as he concludes his instructions to the actors: "To be given an outline upon which you are free to improvise as your talents permit is all the gift any man dare expect of life. All other vauntings are blasphemy."

NOTES

[1] Pierre Louis Duchartre, *The Italian Comedy* (New York: Dover, 1961), p. 161.

[2] Allardyce Nicoll, *The World of Harlequin* (London: Cambridge University Press, 1963), p. 18.

[3] Roger Manvell, *Film* (London: Penguin, 1946), p. 84.

[4] André Bazin, *What Is Cinema?* (Berkeley: University of California Press, 1967), p. 145.

[5] *Fugitive Masks* is about a troupe of commedia dell'arte actors. It was premiered in the summer of 1965 at Barter Repertory Theatre in Virginia; revised, it was produced in April and May of 1968 at Ohio University in Athens. It was inspired as much by my reading Arthur Knight's description of Sennett's Keystone Company while I was in college as by my study of commedia with Russell Green at the same time. In the description of Harlequin, I have paraphrased some lines by Duchartre, one of many scholars who delights in describing Harlequin. (123-34).

[6] Charles Chaplin, *My Autobiography* (New York: Simon and Schuster, 1964), pp. 144-46.

[7] The summer after I had written the shorter, essay version of this book, I made my first trip to Italy. In a Milan movie theater, I watched Italy's favorite comedian Toto in his latest film. The lights at intermission revealed frescoes on the surrounding walls of Charlie and Harlequin together.

[8] See Kathleen M. Lea, *Italian Popular Comedy* (New York: Russell and Russell, 1962), and Henry F. Salerno, trans. and ed., *Scenarios of the Commedia dell'arte* (New York: New York University Press, 1967).

[9] Arthur Knight, *The Liveliest Art* (New York: New American Library, 1959), pp. 39-42.

[10] Quoted in *Film Makers on Film Making*, ed. Harry Geduld (Bloomington: Indiana University Press, 1967), pp. 37-40.

[11] Quoted in A. M. Nagler, *A Source Book in Theatrical History* (New York: Dover, 1952).

[12] Quoted in William Cahn, *Harold Lloyd's World of Comedy* (New York: Duell, Sloan, and Pearce, 1964), p. 63.

[13] John Grierson, "The Logic of Comedy," *Grierson on Documentary* (Berkeley: University of California Press, 1967), p. 58.

[14] Quoted in George Kernodle, *Invitation to the Theatre* (New York: Harcourt, Brace & World, 1967), p. 243.

[15] For more on the influences of commedia dell'arte, see Nicoll, *The World of Harlequin*, pp. 217-23.

[16] Review in *Film Quarterly*, Winter, 1965-66, p. 58.

A SELECTIVE BIBLIOGRAPHY OF BOOKS IN ENGLISH*

Agee, James. "Comedy's Greatest Era," *Agee on Film.* New York: McDowell-Obolensky, 1958.

Allen, Steve. *The Funny Men.* New York: Simon and Schuster, 1956.

Barr, Charles. *Laurel and Hardy.* Berkeley: University of California Press, 1968.

Bazin, André. *What Is Cinema?* Berkeley and Los Angeles: University of California Press, 1967.

Beaumont, Cyril W. *The History of Harlequin.* New York: Benjamin Blom (1926), 1967.

Blesh, Rudi. *Keaton.* New York: Macmillan Company, 1966.

Brownlow, Kevin. *The Parade's Gone By.* New York: Alfred A. Knopf, 1968.

Cahn, William. *Harold Lloyd's World of Comedy.* New York: Duell, Sloan, and Pearce, 1964.

Chaplin, Charles. *My Autobiography.* New York: Simon and Schuster, 1964.

Duchartre, Pierre Louis. *The Italian Comedy.* New York: Dover (1929), 1966.

Durgnat, Raymond. *The Crazy Mirror: Hollywood Comedy and the American Image.* New York: Horizon Press, 1970.

Everson, William K. *The Art of W. C. Fields.* Indianapolis: Bobbs-Merrill Company, 1967.

Everson, William K. *The Films of Laurel and Hardy.* New York: Cadillac Publishing Company, 1967.

*Original date of publication in parentheses.

Eyles, Allen. *The Marx Brothers: Their World of Comedy.* New York: A. S. Barnes and Company, 1966.

Fowler, Gene. *Father Goose: The Story of Mack Sennett.* New York: Covici Friede, 1934.

Franklin, Joe. *Classics of the Silent Screen.* New York: Citadel Press, 1959.

Geduld, Harry, ed. *Film Makers on Film Making.* Bloomington: Indiana University Press, 1967.

Goldoni, Carlo. *The Comic Theatre.* Lincoln: University of Nebraska Press, (1751) 1969.

Gozzi, Carlo. *Useless Memoirs of Carlo Gozzi.* London: Oxford University Press (1890),1962.

Grierson, John. "The Logic of Comedy." *Grierson on Documentary.* Berkeley and Los Angeles: University of California Press (1947), 1966.

Grotjahn, Martin. *Beyond Laughter.* New York: McGraw-Hill, 1957.

Herrick, Marvin T. *Italian Comedy in the Renaissance.* Urbana and London: University of Illinois Press, 1966.

Huff, Theodore. *Charlie Chaplin.* New York: Henry Schuman, 1951.

Jacobs, Lewis. *The Rise of the American Film.* New York: Harcourt, Brace and Company, 1939

Keaton, Buster, and Charles Samuels. *My Wonderful World of Slapstick.* New York: Doubleday and Company, 1960.

Kennard, Joseph Spencer. *The Italian Theatre.* New York: William Edwin Rudge, 1932.

Knight, Arthur. *The Liveliest Art*. New York: New American Library, 1959.
Lahue, Kalton C. *World of Laughter: The Motion Picture Comedy Short*, 1910-1930. Norman: University of Oklahoma Press, 1966.
Lea, Kathleen M. *Italian Popular Comedy*, 2 vols. New York: Russell and Russell (1934), 1962.
Lebel, J. P. *Buster Keaton*. New York: A. S. Barnes and Company, 1967.
Madden, David. "Harlequin's Sitck, Charlie's Cane," *Film Quarterly*, Fall, 1968.
Madden, David. Review of *My Autobiography*, [Chaplin] *Film Quarterly*, Winter, 1965-66.
Manville, Roger. *Film*. London: Penguin, 1946.
McCabe, John. *Mr. Laurel and Mr. Hardy*. New York: Doubleday and Company, 1961.
McCaffrey, Donald W. *4 Great Comedians: Chaplin, Lloyd, Keaton, Langdon*. New York: A. S. Barnes and Company, 1968.
McDonald, Gerlad D., *et al.*, eds. *The Films of Charlie Chaplin*. New York: Bonanza Books, 1965.
Montgomery, John. *Comedy Films*. London: George Allen and Unwin, 1952.
Nagler, A. M. *A Source Book in Theatrical History*. New York: Dover, 1952.
Nathan, George Jean. *The Popular Theatre*. New York: Alfred A. Knopf, 1918.
Nicoll, Allardyce. *Film and Theatre*. New York: Thomas Y. Crowell, Company, 1936.
Nicoll, Allardyce. *Masks, Mimes and Miracles*. New York: Cooper Square Publishers (1931), 1963.

Nicoll, Allardyce. *The World of Harlequin*. London: Cambridge University Press, 1963.

Niklaus, Thelma. *Harlequin Phoenix: Or The Rise and Fall of a Bergamask Rogue*. London: Bodley Head, 1956.

Oreglia, Giacomo. *The Commedia dell'arte*. London: Methuen and Company (1961), 1968.

Pandolfi, Vita. *La commedia dell'arte: Storia e testo*. 5 vols. Florence, (   ) 1957-60. Not in English, but especially well illustrated.

Ramsaye, Terry. *A Million and One Nights*. New York: Simon and Schuster (1926), 1964.

Robinson, David. *Buster Keaton*. Bloomington and London: Indiana University Press, 1969.

Robinson, David. *The Great Funnies: A History of Film Comedy*. New York: Dutton, 1969.

Rotha, Paul, with Richard Griffin. *The Film Till Now*. New York: Twayne (1949), 1960.

Salerno, Henry F., trans. and ed. *Scenarios of the Commedia dell'arte*. New York: New York University Press, 1967.

Seldes, Gilbert. *The Public Arts*. New York: Simon and Schuster, 1956.

Sennett, Mack, as told to Cameron Shipp. *King of Comedy*. New York: Doubleday, 1964.

Smith, Albert E. and Phil Koury. *Two Reels and a Crank*. New York: Doubleday and Company, 1952.

Smith, Winifred. *The Commedia dell'arte*. New York: Benjamin Blom (1912), 1964.